PARROT PARENTING

How to Provide the Best Care for Your Bird

Samantha Khela

Copyright © 2023 Samantha Khela

All rights reserved.

I want to express my deepest gratitude to all the clients who have generously provided me with invaluable feedback and shared their practical experiences. Their insights greatly assisted me in writing this book, and I am humbled by their trust in me. Being a bird owner myself has taught me the intricacies of their care. The community has been a rich source of knowledge and insights for me. I continue to learn and improve my skills in handling and caring for birds, not only for my clients but also for my own beloved flock.

Furthermore, I would like to pay tribute to my first budgie, Matcha, for introducing me to the joys of bird-keeping and nurturing my love and passion for these magnificent creatures. Although Matcha has passed on, her legacy lives on through my business and my current flock, which includes Maui, Mango, Miko, Apollo, Achilles, Asia, Alesso, and Algarve. I am grateful for the lessons they continue to teach me every day.

I am thankful to my family, especially my mom and dad, who have always given their loving hand for my birds while I'm away. They have selflessly provided them with the love and care that my birds needed when I couldn't.

Lastly, I extend my heartfelt thanks to my husband, Amir Khela, for his unwavering love and support. He has been a pillar of strength throughout my journey, and I could not have achieved any of this without him. His constant encouragement and belief in me have been my guiding light, and I am blessed to have him by my side as I strive to serve and contribute to the bird community's prosperity and success.

CONTENTS

Foreword i

Disclaimer iii

1. Introduction 5
2. Types of Birds 17
3. Bird Cages & Accessories 36
4. Bird Diet... 52
5. Bird's Well-being 72
6. Behavior & Training 112
7. Bird Grooming 128
8. Supportive Products 144

Conclusion 152

Appendices 159

FOREWORD

I am honored to introduce "Parrot Parenting", a book by my wife, Samantha Khela. As a proud husband and a witness to her passion and dedication to birds, I am thrilled to see her share her bird knowledge and experience in this book.

In just the last two years, Samantha has personally cared for over 900 birds, showcasing her vast and remarkable experience with a variety of birds. Samantha has dedicated over 60 hours a week, Monday to Sunday, from dawn to dusk, to caring for birds since 2021, allowing her to gain a level of practical, real-world bird experience that most never attain in their lifetimes. Samantha has been actively involved in the bird community and has always gone above and beyond to give value to both her clients and members of the bird community. Through her dedication and tireless efforts, she has gained the trust and respect of fellow bird owners and enthusiasts and has become a valued member of the bird-loving community.

Having witnessed Samantha's profound love and respect for birds, I can attest to her unwavering commitment and inspiring dedication to their well-being. Her expertise and knowledge in bird care are unrivaled, and I am proud to see her share them with the world through this book.

I wholeheartedly recommend "Parrot Parenting" to all bird lovers, whether you are a first-time parrot parent or a seasoned owner. Within these pages, you'll discover insights that not only elevate the quality of care for your bird but also transform you into an informed bird owner. The book prioritizes your bird's safety and strengthening your bond with your bird through greater mutual understanding.

Sincerely,

Amir Khela

DISCLAIMER

The content in this book is intended to provide helpful information on the subjects discussed for educational and informational purposes only. It is not intended, nor should it be used, to diagnose or treat any medical conditions. Neither the author nor the publisher assumes any responsibility for any actions taken or not taken as a result of reading this book, and they are not liable for any damages or negative consequences resulting from any action or inaction by any person who reads or follows the information in this book. The references provided are for informational purposes only and do not constitute an endorsement of any websites or other sources. Readers should also be aware that the websites and businesses listed in this book may change or become obsolete over time. The reader assumes all responsibility and accountability for the use of this information, and neither the author nor the publisher assumes any responsibility for errors, omissions, or differing interpretations of the subject matter.

1. INTRODUCTION

"Matcha unfortunately passed, and she had passed prematurely due to a poor diet, which was entirely my wrongdoing. This was what inspired me to really learn about avian care and how to take better care of birds."

As a fellow bird owner, I understand how much we love our feathered friends. They are so little, yet they bring us so much joy and happiness, and we only want the best for them. However, sometimes providing the best care for our pets can be a challenge.

I often see bird owners who do not know how to provide the best possible care for their pets simply due to a lack of knowledge. Ignorance is not bliss. I have personally experienced a premature loss due to my lack of knowledge.

Moreover, even when bird owners are aware of the care their birds need, busy schedules can often prevent us from delivering the quality care they truly deserve.

This book is a guide to help bird owners overcome these challenges and become better caregivers for their pets. Whether you're a new bird owner or you have years of experience, this book will provide you with the knowledge and tools you need to provide the best possible care for your feathered friend. I hope that by the time you finish reading this book, you will understand your bird in a deeper way and build a greater loving connection with your bird.

From learning about your bird's nutritional needs to creating a stimulating environment and building a strong bond with your bird, this book covers everything you need to know to be a responsible and loving bird owner.

I wrote this book because I understand the struggles that bird owners face when it comes to caring for their pets. In the last 2 years, serving over 900 bird owners in Toronto, I've witnessed recurring scenarios that prompted me to write this book. These include a death by accidental starvation of a budgie switching from seeds to pellets, a lovebird flying out of an open window, and a jenday conure feather plucking due to a lack of stimulation and attention, among others. With this guide, I hope to make the process of caring for your bird a little easier and more enjoyable. After all, our birds give us so much love and happiness, and they deserve nothing less than the best from us.

I don't know how versed you are with birds, but you do not necessarily have to read this book sequentially. The chapters in the book are clearly labeled, allowing you to easily jump to sections of interest.

Note: Although parrots belong to a specific group of birds, I use birds and parrots interchangeably throughout the book.

◆◆◆

From Nest to Narrative, How It All Started

1. Samantha Khela

My name is Samantha Khela, and my educational background is in Public Policy. I earned my master's from the Munk School of Global Affairs and Public Policy at the University of Toronto.

When I began my master's program, I took an internship at the Department of National Defence in Ottawa. I had recently moved out of Toronto for the first time, and living alone at the time, I was eager to have a pet companion. After trying pet rabbits and fish without luck, I finally found a good fit with a parakeet (budgie) I named Matcha.

Matcha was a feisty little budgie that I absolutely

adored. I cherished Matcha deeply. She supported me during that summer in Ottawa and through various milestones over the three years we spent together.

Unfortunately, Matcha passed away prematurely due to my oversight in her diet, which was entirely my wrongdoing. This was what inspired me to really learn about avian care and how to take better care of birds.

2. *Matcha*

Our Flock's Journey, The Story of Our Flock

3. Maui

Before Matcha's untimely passing, I wanted to find her a companion, especially for times when I was busy with work.

When I was back in Toronto, I adopted Maui from a young girl in Scarborough, who had quite a flock herself. I adopted Maui when she was just a few weeks old. Initially, I even mistook her for a boy!

4. Mango & Maui

Maui and Matcha actually bonded successfully, but only to be cut short once Matcha succumbed to her underlying illness. So when Matcha passed, I knew I had to get Maui a partner. Together with my then-boyfriend (now husband), we brought Mango, the budgie, into our lives. This little guy was so small and innocent - and he took to Maui very well!

For a while, I cared for Maui and Mango on my own because my partner and I didn't live together until we got married. I adore my two budgies, but after some research, I realized the interaction I received from them was minimal. I yearned for a pet bird that would thrive on human affection and attention.

5. The Original BST Family

My research led me to the green cheeked conure as the perfect fit, particularly because these birds are sociable, much more so than budgies. As a special wedding gift to ourselves, we welcomed Miko, a yellow-sided green cheek conure with a high red factor, into our family.

6. Algarve, Alesso, Asia and Achilles

I thought this had completed my flock, however Mango and Maui had hit it off so well that they had four baby budgies, named Algarve, Alesso, Asia, and Achilles. Raising these baby birds was an incredible experience.

At that time, my family teased me that adopting another bird would make me a *crazy bird lady*. However, Miko had befriended our temporary resident, Apollo. They became so close that they were now a role model pair. When Apollo's plans to go to the United States fell through, he was going to be left without a home. Without hesitation, I decided to welcome what I *believe* to be the final member of our flock, adopting our newest bird.

7. The whole BST Family

Bird Sitting Toronto, Toronto's Parrot Paradise

First and foremost, I am neither a veterinarian nor a veterinary technician.

In writing this book, I've drawn from my personal experiences at Bird Sitting Toronto, where I've cared for numerous birds. My insights also come from extensive online research, readings, interactions with veterinarians, and my active involvement in bird community discussions.

I've spent over 5,000 hours interacting with nearly a thousand unique birds. I'm deeply grateful to everyone who entrusted me with their cherished birds.

I'd like to share photos of the clients I've had the privilege to serve over the past two years. **Truly, they've shaped the person I am today.**

On my wall, I proudly display a polaroid of every bird I've had the honor of caring for.

The Bird Sitting Toronto Wall!

8. Polaroids of birds visiting BST

2. TYPES OF BIRDS

"A parrot's love is like a rainbow, beautiful and full of color."

To get to know your bird better, it would help to know the different types of birds. Bird care varies across different species, though many general principles remain the same.

Regardless of the species, basic care principles such as ensuring a safe and enriching environment, providing balanced and proper nutrition, and securing regular medical check-ups are universally essential. Allow me to share detailed insights on the care of birds of various sizes, complemented by **real pictures** I've personally taken, of the diverse and wonderful birds I've had the privilege of nurturing and looking after.

Small Birds

9. Chip and Kip

Budgies, also known as parakeets from Australia, are playful birds with pleasant chirps. Males, like my pet Mango, are more energetic and better speakers than females. With proper care, they can live 10-15 years and are among the most common birds I've cared for.

10. Ion and Rio

Conures, a diverse group with over a dozen types, are outgoing, acrobatic, and intelligent birds. They often attempt cage escapes and can live up to 25 years. They're the species of birds I care for most frequently.

11. Lemonade

Cockatiels are gentle Australian parrots known for their singing and pleasant chirps. While not as timid as budgies or as bold as conures, they can be affectionate. I've cared for many, and with proper care, they can live over 20 years; their chirps are my favorite.

12. George

Lovebirds, originating from Africa, are small birds with cheeky personalities. While males are typically gentle, females can become aggressive during breeding season (their bites hurt!). They can live 15-25 years.

13. Peywacket and Hedwig

Lineolated parakeets, also known as "*linnies*," are known for their friendly, playful personalities. They are generally quiet and social in nature. They can live up to an average lifespan of 10 years. I've cared for dozens of linnies and they've always been a joy to have.

14. Tina and Mimico

Parrotlets are small, energetic but quiet parrots that are known for their vibrant colors and playful personalities. Although they are small in size, they are intelligent and can be taught to do tricks. Parrotlets can live for 15 to 20 years with proper care. I've cared for over a dozen parrotlets and even owned one of my own in the past. They are so cute!

Medium Birds

15. Barfi

Pionus Parrots, known for their colorful plumage and gentle nature, are ideal for apartment living due to their quietness. They come in various species and can live 25-40 years. Having cared for several, I've found them to be calm and gentle.

16. Nike and Luka

Caiques, vibrant parrots from South America, are playful and intelligent, best suited for engaged adults. With proper care, they live up to 30 years but can be quite vocal. From my experience with a dozen Caiques, each has a distinct personality.

17. Lucky

Quakers or monk parakeets from South America are affectionate, playful, and mischievous pets. Requiring ample stimulation, they can live 20-30 years and can be loud and noisy! Every Quaker I've cared for has been very energetic.

18. Kiwi

Senegal parrots from West Africa's forests are calm birds that bond closely with owners, making them perfect for apartments. With a lifespan of 25-30 years, they're less common; however, the few I've cared for have been serene and adorable!

19. Beeboy

Indian Ringneck Parakeets are a larger type of parakeets. They are smart and capable of mimicking human speech better than most parrots. As pets, they tend to be less affectionate and are less likely to enjoy physical contact. Ringneck Parakeets can live between 15 to 25 years. I love caring for Indian Ringnecks, it's always fascinating to speak with them. However, they can be very noisy!

Large Birds

20. Toto

Alexandrine Parakeets are larger parrots known for their striking plumage and ringed necks. Renowned for their ability to mimic, they're sociable and can form strong bonds with their caregivers. They live for about 20-30 years. I've only interacted with a handful.

21. Babyface

Congo African Greys, native to the rainforests of West and Central Africa, are celebrated for their exceptional intelligence and mimicry skills. With a silver-grey plumage, they are often considered one of the most intelligent birds. They can live up to 50 years, and every African Grey I've cared for has showcased unique mimicry.

22. Zafran

Lorikeets, with their rainbow-colored feathers, are nectar-eating parrots native to the Australasian region. They are lively, playful, and known for their acrobatic antics. With a lifespan of 15-20 years, the few lorikeets I've cared for have been very loud!

23. Sparky and Ginger

Eclectus parrots are unique, the males are green, and females are red. Known for their calm and gentle nature, they are great companions. Living up to 30 years, the eclectus I've cared for have been gentle giants.

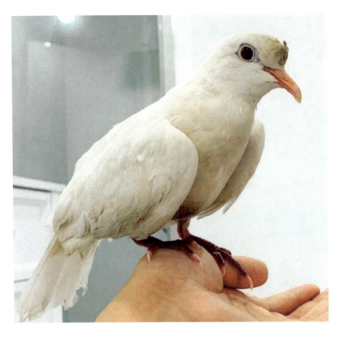

24. Kook

Doves, with their soft coos and gentle demeanor, are symbols of peace. These birds are often found in both wild and urban settings. With a lifespan of 10-15 years, I've cared for only one Dove, which the owner has now informed me has passed away.

25. Klaus

Pigeons, often seen in the city, are versatile and adaptable birds. They have a remarkable homing instinct and have been used historically for communication. They live up to 6-15 years. Although they're plentiful on the streets, I've only cared for two different pigeons.

26. Bobo

Cockatoos, native to Australia and Indonesia, are recognizable by their showy crests and loud vocalizations. They are sociable, intelligent, and can be quite affectionate with their human companions. With a lifespan of 40-60 years, the 2 Cockatoos I've cared for have been uniquely different from the other birds. Bobo, the bird shown below who was reaching close to 40 years of age, has unfortunately passed away this year.

3. BIRD CAGES & ACCESSORIES

"Many people spend months preparing for a major home purchase but often choose a birdcage without much thought."

When my husband and I moved into our first condo; we spent six months searching for the perfect home. Yet, when it came to buying a new cage for our birds, we made a decision in just ten minutes on Amazon.

Many people spend months preparing for a major home purchase but often choose a birdcage without much thought. Given that your pet bird will spend most of its time in this cage, it's important to select a cage more carefully and one that's truly right for them.

◆◆◆

Housing Your Bird: Cage Considerations

Aesthetics

For many bird owners, cage aesthetics is the primary concern. While a stylish cage might enhance your home's appearance, its visual appearance does not benefit your bird. Birds value functionality over aesthetics. A visually appealing cage can strain your bond if your bird dislikes it, or if it's challenging for you to maintain. Remember the adage, *"don't judge a book by its cover"* and don't choose a cage based solely on its looks.

Cage Size & Shape

The cage is your bird's entire world, so it's important to get them the biggest cage reasonably possible that is within your budget and living space means. It's best to avoid using round cages because they don't have corners for your bird to retreat to and it may cause unnecessary stress. Rectangular cages are a better choice for creating great layouts because they provide more space for your bird to move horizontally.

As a general rule of thumb, the width of the cage is more important than the height for birds.

The spacing between the bars is an aspect to factor in. It should be narrow enough to prevent escapes or injuries but appropriate for the bird size. I've seen budgies trying to slip through gaps meant for larger birds. While I haven't witnessed any harm firsthand, it's a scenario best avoided.

Cage Features & Functionalities

Bird cages can come with a variety of features. Here are six key features to consider when choosing the right cage for you and your feathered companion:

1. **Food and Water Compartment**: A section allowing you to access the food or water bowl without opening the cage's main entrance. It helps to quickly change the food and water without interfering with your bird's personal space. Your bird will likely not be able to make their grand performance and strategically escape while you're changing the food and water.

2. **Pull-Out Bottom Tray**: Common in modern cages, this feature streamlines the cleaning process. It becomes seamless to take out and

replace the bottom lining.

3. **Seed Catchers**: Seed catchers come in two forms: nets that wrap around the cage, and built-in trays that protrude outward, taking up additional space. While they minimize the mess, I find the minor reduction in fallen seeds is not worth it for me personally when I already clean several times a day.

4. **Playtops**: These are areas above the cage for birds to play. They can be custom-made with toys or integrated into the cage. Playtops help me contain the mess as the cage liner will capture the bird droppings.

5. **Wheels**: Especially in heavier cages, wheels facilitate movement around the home.

6. **Storage Space**: Many medium-to-large cages offer storage beneath for bird supplies.

These are functions that you can use strategically to make the process of caring for your bird more convenient.

Sometimes I get a cage that doesn't have a pull-out food and water compartment. If your cage does not them, an alternative is to use water bottles and insert them from the outside.

27. Water bottle for Food or Water

The easier you make it for yourself to change the food and water, the more likely you will do it without thinking it's a chore.

Cage Placement

In general, the living room is an excellent location to place a bird cage because it is a room that is often used by the family, which can help keep the bird well-socialized and entertained. However, if you choose to put the cage in the kitchen, be wary for the potential dangers such as gas leaks from old refrigerators, fumes from Teflon-coated pans, hot stoves, open windows and doors, as well as other hazards. It is important to be cautious and take steps to ensure the safety of your bird in the kitchen.

> *I've once received a call from a desperate bird owner frantically asking what to do about his bird who got severely burnt on the kitchen stove. It was such a sad circumstance, because all I can recommend is to immediately go see his veterinarian and I can't help but picture myself in the same helpless scenario with any of my birds.*

A wise decision is to make sure that the cage is backed against a solid wall because birds are prey animals and constantly feeling the need to *"watch their back"* can be stressful for them. Finally, keep in mind that birds feel safe when they are up high, so placing the cage higher up will be stress-relieving.

Birds will require a safe environment where they can rest at ease. Most parrots originate near the equator where it is dark for 10-12 hours each night, so depriving them of a sleep period shorter than this can be negative for their health.

If the cage is placed in a quiet location away from disturbances, a cover may not be necessary. However, if you do choose to cover the cage at night to protect your bird from cold drafts or to block out light and noise, be sure to leave room for ventilation.

I take extra precautions with cockatiels because they are prone to night frights— which are intense panic episodes that can cause them to frantically try to escape perceived threats. However, because they are caged, their frantic attempts to escape during these frights can result in self-injury by hitting the cage walls.

I generally cover all cockatiels at night to reduce the chance of night fright by eliminating visual scares. I also go out of my way to eliminate any loud sounds that might scare them at night. Leaving a night light on also helps!

Cage Lining

To keep your bird's cage clean, line the bottom with disposable paper such as newspaper or paper towels. You can throw these away daily to maintain a hygienic environment for your bird. Modern newsprint is lead-free and non-toxic for birds, even if they chew on it. Avoid using sandpaper cage liners sold in pet stores, as birds may ingest the sand and develop intestine obstructions.

Avoid using wood chips, shavings, clay, cat litter, shredded or recycled paper, or corncob bedding as cage lining for birds. These materials can be harmful and unsafe for a variety of reasons. For example, wood chips and shavings can contain harmful chemicals, clay and cat litter can accumulate harmful bacteria. Corncob bedding can be ingested by birds and may cause digestive issues. To keep your bird safe and healthy, it is best to keep it simple and use disposable paper like newspaper or paper towels as the cage lining.

Cleaning

We don't want our birds to get sick, nor do we want to deal with any bugs. Therefore, regular cleaning is important. The frequency depends on your schedule, your birds' cleanliness, and room conditions like temperature and humidity.

Maintain your cage hygiene by washing it with soap and hot water. Ideally the wash is done weekly, but if not possible, ensure a deep clean monthly.

Clean both the food and water dishes daily to avoid bacterial buildup. Even if water appears clean, a used bowl will be slimy to touch.

Cleaning the cage with soap and warm water is sufficient to remove fecal and food debris and prevent the growth of bacteria. Disinfecting the cage is only necessary if the bird has been sick or if you are adding a new bird to a previously used cage. Overusing disinfectants and chemicals can be harmful to your bird.

When disinfecting, let the solution sit for at least 15 minutes before scrubbing and rinsing. Make sure to rinse off thoroughly to avoid leaving harmful residues in the cage.

Toy Types, Keeping Your Bird Entertained

The best toys are ones that have a variety of different coloured and textured materials hanging on a chain or rope. The different types of bird toys include, but is not limited to:

- Chewing toys
- Climbing toys
- Perches & swings
- Noise making toys
- Puzzles
- Play gyms
- Foraging toys

Chewing Toys

28. A Chewable Toy providing entertainment (AI)

Chewable bird toys are specifically designed to be easily torn apart by birds. Doing so will provide your bird with a sense of accomplishment and will keep them entertained. Chewing and tearing up toys will also help to keep their beak healthy.

I find that birds seem to enjoy the attention they receive from their human caregivers when they destroy a toy and have them clean up afterwards!

Foraging Toys

29. A Foraging Toy instigating curiosity (AI)

Foraging toys mimic the natural behaviour of birds in the wild, allowing them to search for food. A diverse range of foraging toys are available, and I particularly like those made from indestructible plastic for durability. However, certain foraging toys are designed to be destroyed, revealing hidden treats inside for your bird. Foraging toys are a great source of mental stimulation for your birds. The less time you can dedicate to your birds, the more valuable these toys become.

Exercise Toys

30. Exercise Toy promoting activity (AI)

While wild birds fly miles a day and get their exercise, domesticated birds don't have that opportunity and engage in far less physical activity. Although it's not a complete substitute, exercise toys such as swings, climbing ladders, or ropes can help build your bird's balance and strength.

Bird Emergency, Avian First Aid Kit

First aid kits have saved many human lives during emergencies. Similarly, an avian first aid kit can be important in times of emergency for your bird. In emergencies, situations are time-sensitive, leaving no room to search for or buy items. It doesn't help that we usually act frantically during emergencies.

While having an avian first aid kit is essential, it is equally important to know how to use the supplies within it.

This kit, by no means, is a replacement for a veterinarian; it is designed to stabilize your bird until they can be professionally assessed and taken care of by an avian veterinarian.

You need to have your veterinarian and poison control emergency contacts in your avian first aid kit. Keeping all the phone contacts handy can be a lifesaver during emergencies.

You will need to have a bird carrier at home if your bird's cage is not easily transportable. A bird carrier is great for immediate transport or when confinement in a smaller space is necessary to restrict movement and further injury.

31. Bird First Aid Kit

Here is what I keep in my DIY avian first aid kit.

Item	Utility
Hand Towel	To hold the bird without using your hands directly.
Gauze	For covering wounds.
Flour	To stop further bleeding.
Cotton Balls	For applying solutions in small amounts.
Q-Tips	For cleaning out small wounds.
Micropore Tape	To hold the gauze in place.
Penlight	To provide light for examination.
Syringe	To feed birds formula when sick.
Betadine	Solution to clean wounds.
Latex Gloves	To prevent the spread of germs.
Vet Contact information	Veterinarian and poison control centre phone numbers.
Sticks	To immobilize broken limbs.
Hydrogen Peroxide	Helps to remove blood from feathers.

4. BIRD DIET

"From the smallest parakeets to the largest macaws, from the fruit-loving eclectus to the nut-craving African grey, understanding what to feed your bird is important."

As a parrot parent, your primary responsibility is to ensure your bird's diet is balanced and nutritious. A bird's diet goes far beyond the typical birdseed mix found in most pet stores. For optimal health, birds need a varied diet that includes fruits, vegetables, grains, proteins, and essential supplements with each component playing a unique role. From the smallest parakeets to the largest macaws, from the fruit-loving eclectus to the nut-craving African grey, understanding what to feed your bird is important.

Let's delve into the various aspects of a bird's diet to enhance the quality of care you can offer to your feathered companion by becoming a well-informed bird owner.

Seeds vs. Pellets, A Parrot's Diet Dilemma

Birds can enjoy a well-rounded diet comprising of both pellets and seeds, but the consensus advice emphasizes that pellets should constitute the majority (70-80%) of their nutritional intake. This is because pellets offer a more complete range of nutrients for your bird's well-being, including vital vitamins and minerals.

32. Seeds high in fat (AI)

On the other hand, seeds are high in fat and are often an inadequate source of nutrients. While it's acceptable to give seeds as an occasional treat or supplement, they should not form the main component of your bird's diet.

Consider your bird's ability to fly. If their wings are clipped, they won't fly much or burn as many calories. Adjust their diet by reducing seed intake for a better balance.

In the wild, birds cover vast distances in search of their next meal, making seeds an excellent energy source. However, our domesticated birds lack the luxury of such free flight and don't burn nearly the same amount of calories.

Much like the way the modernization of America resulted in a prolonged surplus of calorie intake, leading to obesity and health issues, a similar scenario may unfold with our domesticated birds.

Obesity in parrots can lead to several health problems, including:

- **Arthritis**: Excess weight places additional stress on the joints, which can lead to arthritis, causing pain and difficulty with mobility.
- **Liver disease**: Obesity in birds can cause liver disease, which can result in reduced liver function and potentially fatal liver failure.

- **Respiratory problems**: Obesity can make it harder for birds to breathe properly, leading to respiratory difficulties, such as shortness of breath and wheezing.

- **Reproductive problems**: Overweight birds can have trouble laying eggs and may have difficulty reproducing.

- **Decreased lifespan**: Obesity in birds can lead to a reduced lifespan, as the additional weight and associated health problems can shorten their lives.

- **Behavioral problems**: Overweight birds may become lethargic and less active, leading to a decline in their overall health and quality of life.

I made the mistake of giving my first budgie, Matcha, a seed only diet for several years which led to her unfortunate premature death by liver disease. Matcha's passing was the reason why I picked up several books on birds and studied how to provide better care for birds. Matcha is the reason why I try my best to educate others, so they don't repeat my mistakes.

Switching to Pellets, Making the Dietary Switch

33. Nutritious Pellets (AI)

Seeds were the go-to, affordable option for feeding pet birds without much thought. Now, it's widely understood that seeds lack crucial vitamins and minerals like Vitamin A and Calcium. Now that you understand the distinction between seeds and pellets, you might be pondering how to make this transition. When you do try to make the change for the better, you encounter the real problem with seeds is that most birds won't eat anything else when they're given free access to seeds.

Similar to a child pushing aside broccoli to savor french fries, most birds will selectively pick out their preferred seed and use their beaks to toss the rest of the seeds and pellets out of the dish.

So how can you make the switch to pellets?

There are two methods of achieving the switch successfully. The first is to mix pellets into the seed, gradually reducing the amount of seed until only pellets are given. This is the method I have the most experience with.

How the gradual transition is done

1. **The Pellet Introduction**: Begin by sprinkling a small amount of these pellets into their regular seed mix for a few weeks. You can be creative to speed up the process. Hand-feed them, add pellets to their fresh fruits and veggies, or casually scatter some on a table when they're out and about.

2. **Adjusting the Ratio**: After the bird has acquainted itself with the pellets, initiate the shift in the seed-to-pellet ratio. Do this gradually, meaning, decrease the seeds and up the pellets slowly. The goal is to have them finish off the seeds while maintaining an interest in nibbling on the pellets.

3. **Watchful Observation**: As you observe, you'll see the bird engaging with the pellets—whether for a playful toss or a taste test. This is the cue for a slight adjustment. Provide a small portion of seeds in their regular dish while situating a dish of pellets closer to their favorite spot. You'll notice their growing affinity for pellets when you spot changes in the color and texture of their droppings or discover crumbled pellets at the bottom of the dish.

4. **Unity in Flock:** If you're a proud caretaker of a flock, this transition will likely be quicker. Birds tend to eat more when there's a little friendly competition. So, don't be surprised if the pellets disappear faster when you've got more than one beak to feed. It's a chain reaction, essentially. One starts pecking, and the rest swiftly join in.

This is how my flock of six budgies quickly started eating bird chop. It didn't take long for them to adapt; as they observed each other pecking at it, eating became a competitive activity. Now, they race to get the chop every time I introduce it.

5. **Goodbye Seeds**: At last, the moment has come to bid farewell to seeds. However, patience is key. Aim for a smooth transition. So, gradually cut back on the seeds until they're completely off the menu. Monitor your bird's droppings and overall behavior throughout this period. A healthy bird is a happy bird. If you notice anything unusual—like a lack of droppings or significant changes in behavior—do not hesitate to seek advice from a veterinarian.

6. **Patience Pays Off**: This can be frustrating if it's taking longer than we expected. But remember, *Rome wasn't built in a day*. Patience and persistence are key in this transition. The ultimate goal is to ensure your birds are getting all the nutrients they need for a healthy life. So, keep monitoring their progress and tweak your approach if necessary.

The second method is to monitor the droppings and switch your bird directly to pellets, going *"cold turkey"*.

How Cold Turkey Is Done

1. **Perfect Timing**: Timing is everything. We wouldn't want to stress our bird with diet changes right after a major upheaval, such as a move, an illness, a new cage, or a change of ownership. Therefore, look for a couple of peaceful days when life is as routine as it can be.

2. **The First Day - Clean Slate**: Begin the day by thoroughly cleaning the cage, eliminating any visible seeds. Substitute them with pellets. Line the cage's bottom with fresh newspaper. This will help you in closely monitoring the droppings.

3. **Bird Poop Detective**: You're going to see some changes in the droppings throughout the day. Initially, they should look normal - mostly green with a hint of white. However, if your bird delays trying the new food, you'll notice their droppings reducing in size with less green. The green part signifies food in their system. Keep a close watch!

4. **The Second Day - Observation Continues**: You're likely to wake up to a sight of scattered and crumbled pellets. While this could just mean your bird had some playtime, it could also mean they had a taste. Check the newest droppings. Are they larger with more green? If yes, then we might be making progress. However, don't rush into putting seeds back just yet. We don't want

to risk a seed relapse. Continue monitoring the droppings for a few more days.

5. **Plan B**: If you wake up on day two to find the droppings still tiny, or if you spot two or three all-white droppings in a row, it's best to stop. These are signs that your bird's digestive system is empty. Immediately reintroduce seeds and wait at least a week before reattempting. The last thing we want is to risk starvation.

This serves as a general guide, drawn from my personal experience. Keep in mind that every bird is unique and may react differently. If your bird displays signs of distress or if you have any concerns during the diet transition, seek immediate advice from an avian veterinarian. It's always better to be safe and provide the best care for your bird.

Filtered vs. Tap, What's The Best Water for Your Bird

34. Conure drinking water (AI)

It is important to provide your bird daily fresh water. Parrots are highly dependent on water for their survival and must have access to clean, fresh water at all times. Unlike certain other birds, parrots do not have the ability to store water in their bodies, so they need a continual supply.

As a general rule, parrots should never go more than 24 hours without access to water.

Prolonged dehydration can lead to serious health problems, including organ damage and death.

Whether filtered or tap water is best for your parrot depends on the quality of the tap water in your area.

If your tap water contains elevated levels of chlorine, heavy metals, or other contaminants, using filtered water becomes important. Parrots, being more sensitive than humans to contaminants, benefit from a cleaner water source. Conversely, if your tap water meets drinking water standards and is of high quality, it is likely safe for your parrot.

Additionally, it's crucial to recognize that some parrots may be sensitive to changes in their water source. Therefore, if you decide to transition from tap water to filtered water, it's best to make the change gradually, allowing your bird time to adjust.

In Toronto, the city where I reside, there is a high standard for water quality. Nevertheless, the water supplied by the city undergoes the building's pipes, which may not uphold the same standard as the city. Due to the numerous factors beyond my control in this process, I prefer to give filtered water to birds in my care.

Feathered Foes, Foods Not Safe for Birds

While it's important to know what foods parrots can safely eat, understanding the ones that can be toxic is equally important. In general, it's advisable to avoid foods high in salt, fat, sugars, or those containing dyes or preservatives. Here are 11 items to consistently keep off their menu:

1. **Raw meat**: Avoid raw meat as it may contain bacteria harmful to birds.

2. **Fruit seeds**: Most fruit seeds, such as apple and pear seeds, contain cyanogenic glycosides that can be toxic in large quantities.

3. **Mushrooms**: Some mushroom species are toxic to birds and should be avoided.

4. **Alcohol**: Alcohol can cause liver and brain damage, leading to death in birds.

5. **Avocado**: Avocados contain persin, which is toxic and can cause respiratory distress and death.

6. **Onion**: Onions contain sulfoxides and disulfides, which can damage red blood cells, leading to anemia.

7. **Caffeine**: Caffeine can cause hyperactivity, irregular heartbeats, and death in birds.

8. **High salt**: Excessive salt intake can lead to rapid dehydration and electrolyte imbalances. Canned foods often have a high salt composition.

9. **Garlic**: Garlic contains sulfoxides and disulfides, potentially causing damage to red blood cells and leading to anemia.

10. **Dairy**: While small amounts of dairy may be acceptable, parrots lack the enzyme lactase, making most dairy products likely to draw fluids into the digestive tract and cause diarrhea.

11. **Chocolate**: Chocolate contains theobromine, which can be toxic to birds, causing seizures, vomiting, and heart problems.

35. Unsafe bird food (AI)

Grit & Gravel, Necessary for Your Bird?

Grit refers to tiny bits of stones or rocks, like gravel, and it was believed that all birds required grit for proper digestion. This topic of whether parrots require grit or gravel in their diet has been widely debated for years. Despite being controversial, most avian veterinarians currently state that the risks of using gravel outweigh any benefits. They advise not to use it at all, emphasizing that grit is not necessary for the dietary needs of parrots.

The reason why parrots should avoid eating grit is that it can clog their digestive system. Additionally, their intestinal openings are small, making it harder for them to excrete grit. Unlike other birds, parrots don't need grit for digestion as they have powerful and well-developed gizzards (bird stomach).

Your parrot may still willingly eat grit to fulfill its mineral requirements, particularly calcium, which is important for healthy bones and egg formation. However, a parrot eating more grit than usual could indicate that it has mineral deficiencies or imbalances in its diet. Instead of relying on grit, the safer option is to add a cuttlebone to its diet, which will provide the necessary calcium.

I used to include grit in my avian first aid kit because I believed it was helpful for digestion. I would give it to my first budgie, Matcha. I never noticed a difference before and after feeding, and I would naively provide grit, thinking I was offering the best for my bird.

36. Parrot eating grit (AI)

Parrot Chop, Nourishing Your Bird

You can include chop as part of your bird's balanced diet. Chop refers to a processed or finely chopped mixture of vegetables, fruits, nuts, seeds, cooked grains, and other ingredients that can provide essential nutrients and vitamins for your parrot. However, it's important to ensure that the chop you make or buy does not contain toxic ingredients, as some human food can be harmful to them.

The popularity of chop has increased among pet bird owners due to its health benefits to your pet bird's wellbeing and health.

Chop is a great way to introduce a variety of different foods to your bird's diet. It may seem difficult and time-consuming, as I once thought. However, chop can be made in bulk, stored in the freezer for long periods, and used in tandem with their seeds or pellets.

One single session in the kitchen can provide enough chop supply that will last several months. I generally keep two different types of bird chop to provide a diversity of nutrients. I prefer to place them into ice trays so it's easy to take out a day's dose of chop. It's incorporated into my morning routine, and I don't think about it, just like how I brush my teeth on autopilot.

37. BST Chop packaged to preserve freshness

There are various ways to create your own chop for your pet birds. The general idea is to have everything finely chopped, but not mashed, so your birds can pick through it.

When you are first introducing chop to your bird's diet, I recommend making the mix so that about half of it consists of food your bird is familiar with and enjoys eating. All vegetables (except onion, avocado, and a few more) can be used in their raw form.

Make sure you rinse, coarsely cut, and then process small batches in a food processor on low speed before mixing it all together in a bowl. This will give the chop the proper consistency it needs.

Aim for approximately 50% vegetables, 40% cooked grains and legumes, and 10% dry ingredients. It's not a hard science; there are other ratios that you can follow.

Chop mixes can be as simple or complicated as you want; it's completely up to you! You can copy and paste an existing chop recipe instead of creating your own, especially in the beginning, to build confidence and experience.

The chop mix might seem like foreign cuisine to your bird. They're going to need some help understanding that it's actually food. If your bird has a soft spot for a particular fruit or vegetable, chop it into hearty chunks and top off the chop mix before serving. Your bird might initially just pick out their favorites, but they can't help but get a taste of the rest of the mix in the process.

For birds who do not eat fruit or vegetables yet, a sprinkle of their familiar seed mix into the chop can do the trick. It's like a breadcrumb trail leading them to a healthier lifestyle. Once they get comfortable with this new gastronomic adventure, slowly bring down the seeds.

My birds don't leave any chop behind; they love to compete over the chop, and it's a rewarding sight to see my birds eating so healthily. Chop has been so successful for my flock that I started making chop in bulk and delivering it straight to bird owners' homes!

38. Jackson eating chop

I call it **Parrot's Plate**; it's essentially bird chop I make from home and portion into daily pieces that are designed to be convenient and easy to serve. I deliver across the Greater Toronto Area, and I'm proud to contribute to the health of all the birds that eat my chop!

Read More: https://birdsittingtoronto.ca/parrots-plate/

5. BIRD'S WELL-BEING

"Birds are incredible at hiding their symptoms up until the very end."

I still vividly recall the heartbreaking moment when my first budgie, Matcha, died in my hands. She experienced spasms before flopping over to her side on Wednesday, December 2, 2020, in my room in Brampton. Seeing her lifeless in my hands has left a big impact on me.

39. Matcha in 2020

Birds generally do not just die for no reason. They are incredible at hiding their symptoms until the very end when they are very sick. My budgie didn't get sick right away, but it was gradually over time. That's why it's important to keep up with your bird's well-being so that your beloved bird has a long and fruitful life.

Parrot Hazards, Common Injuries and Avoidable Situations

One way of providing better care for your feathered friend is by knowing a list of common injuries that your bird is most susceptible to. By knowing what can harm your pet, you can consciously or subconsciously be mindful of and avoid such scenarios from happening.

Since I started serving the bird community, I have heard treacherous horror stories from other parrot owners. I went back on my message history and collected six stories shared with me.

1. **Story 1**: A tragic incident where a door closed on a conure's head, leading to permanent injury and loss of eyesight.

2. **Story 2**: An unfortunate mishap of accidentally stepping on a cockatiel, resulting in a very long hospital stay.

3. **Story 3**: A sudden, inexplicable change in behavior in a pair of normally friendly conures, leading them to harm each other to the point of drawing blood.

4. **Story 4**: A cockatiel suffering a broken blood feather during a night fright episode, causing

significant blood loss.

5. **Story 5:** I have encountered multiple instances of this all-too-common tale: parrots escaping through open windows or doors and vanishing without a trace. It happens far too often.

6. **Story 6:** Another case of door closing on a parrotlet that was walking innocently on the floor, leading to instant death.

Although these are extreme, let's review a list of common parrot injuries and situations that you can actively avoid. This way, you can better expect the unexpected.

Shelter your bird from these 11 situations and learn how to manage them.

1. **Broken blood feather**: If your bird breaks a blood feather, the simplest remedy might be to pull the feather out. However, to avoid causing further distress or harm, it's highly recommended to take your parrot to a veterinarian.

2. **Cat or dog attack**: In the unfortunate event of a pet attack, rush your bird to the veterinarian immediately for a thorough examination and treatment. If you see any open wounds, apply

styptic powder or cornstarch to stop the bleeding during your trip to the veterinarian. An avian first aid kit can be useful in such situations.

3. **Small wounds or abrasions**: If your bird sustains a minor wound that's not bleeding and isn't caused by another animal, clean the wound with betadine and remove any dirt or feathers using tweezers. If possible, apply a small amount of antibiotic ointment and monitor the wound for a few days. If it's a deeper cut, consult with a veterinarian as it may need further treatment.

4. **Bleeding toenail**: If your bird's toenail starts bleeding due to injury or nail clipping, apply styptic powder or cornstarch to clot the blood and stop the bleeding. If the bleeding continues, a visit to the veterinarian is necessary. Keep a close eye on your bird's behavior for signs of secondary infections.

5. **Burns**: In case of burns, immediately run cold water over the area for several minutes, dry gently with gauze, and apply cold compresses. If the burn is severe, rush your bird to your veterinarian or an emergency clinic. Birds can go into shock from burns, and antibiotics may be needed to prevent infection.

6. **Poisoning**: If you suspect your bird has ingested something toxic, call your veterinarian

immediately. Have your local poison control center phone number readily available. Keep note of the time, as your veterinarian and poison control may need details such as what happened, what's the potential toxin, and any symptoms your bird is showing.

7. **Bites by other birds**: If your bird is bitten by another, leading to a break in the skin and blood loss, a veterinarian should be consulted even if your parrot heals quickly. Antibiotics may be necessary to prevent secondary infections and complications.

8. **Night fright**: Birds can harm themselves during episodes of night fright. To avoid this, cover your bird overnight and keep them in a quiet and calm environment. Minimize unpredictable situations that could trigger fright, like random loud noises. Cockatiels are the most common type of bird I witnessed that get night frights, so I am particularly careful with them.

9. **Hitting windows or mirrors**: To prevent collisions, let your bird play near the windows in a calm setting, or consider partial wing clipping to reduce potential impacts. However, birds sometimes may forget about windows when they need to act quickly or respond hastily to fright. I have added cute bird stickers to the windows in my aviary room to make the windows

more visible.

10. **Flying out open doors and windows**: I have chased my budgie, Matcha, down a ravine in 2019, and it was a terrifying experience that I hope no one else has to go through. Thankfully, Matcha's wings were clipped, so I was able to keep up with her and catch her in my bare hands.

Telling your family and guests at home to avoid opening windows and doors is not a good systemic solution. You cannot rely on others, as it's human nature to make mistakes, and accidents happen all the time.

To prevent your bird from flying out, come up with systemic prevention strategies like screening all windows accessible to your bird, preventing your bird from being in areas with frequently opened doors, and putting warning signs on susceptible windows and doors.

I know about a half dozen fellow bird owners who have experienced a loss like this, and it breaks my heart. It's a difficult situation, and sadly, there's not much I can do to help.

It happens so often that I started a bird lost and found online to assist those who are searching for their beloved birds. The website is http://www.lost-found.birdsittingtoronto.ca/

11. **Splay legs**: Splay legs is a condition affecting very young chicks unable to hold their legs together on slippery surfaces. It can be corrected if detected early by making necessary changes to the chick's environment to prevent recurrence. The legs can be held together with gauze tape, cloth strips, or connected rings, but make sure to avoid constricting blood circulation. Once the legs regain their strength, remove the supports. If not corrected, splay legs can become a permanent condition.

Parrot's Oasis, Are My House Plants Safe For My Parrot

Most bird owners don't know which plants are safe for their birds and which are not. They also may not realize that even their pet bird doesn't know the difference between poisonous plants and safe plants.

40. Budgies interacting with plants (AI)

In the wild, there are specific types of plants that grow in specific climates and regions. Wild parrots know what kinds of plants there are in their geographic region, which they evolved in over thousands of years. Birds learn from the flock and their parents in their native environment about what's safe to eat or not; however, domesticated parrots do not go through this process to learn in captivity.

For example, my conure Miko, originating from the Central and South America region, would not be familiar with plants in Toronto, Canada, where we live. On top of that, modern homes can host plants originating from all over the world.

The general rule of thumb is that if you do not know if the plant is safe for your pet bird, assume it isn't, and don't let them approach it.

A list of plants that are NOT safe

- Avocado
- Azalea
- Dieffenbachia
- Elephant's Ear

- English Ivy
- Holly
- Mistletoe
- Nightshades
- Oleander
- Philodendron
- Poinsettia
- Rhododendron
- Rhubarb

A list of plants that are safe

- Aloe
- African Violet
- Bamboo
- Christmas, Easter Cactus
- Ferns
- Jade Plant
- Palms
- Spider Plant

What is Teflon, The Silent Killer

Polytetrafluoroethylene (PTFE) is a substance commonly found in households due to its use as a non-stick coating on cookware, with Teflon being the most well-known brand name of PTFE-based coatings. Other household sources of PTFE include drip pans, waffle irons, clothing irons, ironing board covers, heating elements, and heat lamps.

When PTFE is heated to over 280°C (536°F), it can release toxic particles and acidic gases which are harmful when inhaled. These gases are colorless and odorless, so you can't tell if there's toxicity in the air.

Thankfully, I have yet to personally hear about any incidents with Teflon, but it's a silent bird killer discussed among the bird community.

Birds are particularly vulnerable to PTFE poisoning. Even if birds are not in the same room where Teflon items are used, they can still be at risk of poisoning. Unfortunately, sudden death may be the only sign of PTFE poisoning. I have three HEPA filters in my home, but unfortunately, they will do nothing to protect my birds when it comes to PTFE.

If your bird gets exposed to PTFE, you might notice signs like agitation, fast or heavy breathing, wheezing, wobbling around, weakness, and even seizures. They might seem sluggish or struggle to stay upright on their perch.

The safest way to prevent PTFE poisoning is to get rid of all non-stick products (most commonly kitchen appliances) containing PTFE from the home. If you can't do that, then at the very least make sure your home is well-ventilated when you use these products—open the windows, crank up the stove fan. Keep your bird out of rooms where you're using PTFE items, like the kitchen or laundry room. Be careful not to overheat or burn your cookware, and never leave it alone while it's on the stove.

41. Teflon cookware (AI)

If you think your bird's been exposed to PTFE fumes, get them out of there and into fresh air as soon as possible, then call your veterinarian. Keep in mind, if your bird is really sick from PTFE, it's going to be a tough road to recovery.

Barfing Birds, Why Is My Parrot Vomiting

Vomiting is a typical occurrence in parrots and can either indicate sickness or, more commonly, be a natural part of courtship or parenting.

Parrots are built differently than us. Their vomit sessions don't involve the gut-wrenching, stomach-churning gymnastics we go through—because they don't have a diaphragm. It's like a parrot party trick; they can throw up whenever they want. Vomiting is part of their daily routine, such as when a mother bird regurgitates food to nourish her chicks.

Birds exhibiting symptoms of illness-related vomiting may display one or more of the following signs.

1. Weakness or lethargy.

2. Fluffed-up feathers.

3. Regurgitation accompanied by mucus and a continuous pumping action of the neck.

4. Seizures.

5. The production of watery, green droppings.

6. In severe cases, sudden death may occur.

These symptoms are alarming and warrant immediate veterinary attention. Birds are great at hiding their illnesses until it's too late, so you may not have a lot of time.

To summarize, bird vomiting can stem from many causes: infectious diseases, metabolic issues, nutritional imbalances, toxicity, obstructions, trauma, allergies, behavioral patterns, or even cancer. However, the most common form of vomiting in parrots is regurgitation, typically for courtship or crop feeding. This is normal parrot behavior and should not display any of the alarming symptoms. Being able to tell between these two types of vomiting is crucial to appropriately understand your bird's behavior and respond appropriately.

Leg Bands on Birds, Safety Considerations

Unsurprisingly, birds are not born with leg bands. They are generally banded for either of the following two reasons.

1. **Identification:** The most common reason for leg banding by breeders is to be able to identify the birds.
2. **Migration:** Leg bands may be required for immigrating into other countries.

Apollo, the conure was initially our resident at Bird Sitting Toronto as he was waiting for his migration documents to finish for his eventual move to the United States from Toronto, Canada. Part of the process was to get Apollo's leg banded and to submit a picture as part of the application for migration. Unfortunately, Apollo was not able to proceed with his migration, but he ended up joining our flock and bonded incredibly with Miko.

42. Apollo's band

However, leg bands don't serve any other utility, and they can get too tight as the bird grows, potentially constricting blood supply. You'll notice swelling if there is a constriction of blood supply, and your bird will likely be in pain.

A leg band is now viewed as an accident waiting to happen. Whether it's blood supply being cut or your pet bird getting the band caught in a toy, it can lead to an eventual problem. The worst-case scenario is your veterinarian having to amputate your bird's banded foot.

I have witnessed a conure leg band getting stuck in cage bars where the conure kept gnawing the foot in an attempt to free their leg and risking injury. Although there haven't been any injuries with leg bands under my supervision, it's a ticking time bomb until something happens.

For housed pet birds, the general recommendation is to have the leg band removed once it is no longer needed. The leg band is removed by cutting under anesthesia at your veterinarian's clinic.

Ill Feathers, Spotting a Sick Bird

Over time, you get to know your birds' behaviors and habits, so if something unusual happens, you may wait to see how it feels. However, waiting could be a fatal mistake. Some diseases are acute and require immediate attention, while others have chronic symptoms that come and go.

Here are some of the most noticeable signs that something might be wrong with your bird.

1. **Changes in sleep patterns:** Your bird is sleeping more than usual, which can be normal for baby birds, but excessive sleep may indicate a problem. Unusual sleeping positions, such as at the bottom of the cage or unsteady perching, is a red flag.

2. **Your bird is quieter than normal**: Your bird is quieter than normal, especially during the usual noisy periods. A sudden decrease in vocal activity without apparent reasons might signal discomfort or illness.

3. **Unusual positioning**: If your bird is too weak to sleep in the usual way, it may perch unsteadily on two feet or sleep on the bottom of the cage. These are both significant red flags.

4. **Your bird has fluffed-up feathers**: Fluffed-up feathers, even during activity, can be a sign of a sick bird. Regular feather puffing is normal for temperature regulation, but continuous fluffing may hint at an underlying issue.

5. **Weight changes**: Your bird has lost weight, especially within a short period. Monitoring your bird's average weight is crucial, as rapid weight loss serves as an objective indicator of illness.

6. **Change in bird droppings:** Changes in droppings, outside of normal variations, should be looked into. Persistent changes may mean health issues.

7. **Tail movement**: Unusual tail movement while breathing could indicate respiratory distress. This includes subtle flicking or pronounced movement. If the bird's tail is hanging downward, it's a sign of illness.

8. **Respiratory symptoms**: Increased sneezing, discolored or wet feathers around the nostrils, or blocked nasal openings may suggest a respiratory infection.

9. **Regurgitation**: While some regurgitation is normal behavior, unexpected vomiting requires immediate attention.

10. **Egg binding**: Female birds displaying signs of weakness or lethargy, especially if they have

been laying eggs, may be suffering from potentially fatal egg binding due to a lack of calcium.

Maui, my budgie, expanded our flock by four chicks, and in the subsequent breeding season, I discouraged her egg laying. However, she laid a few empty eggs, and I observed signs of weakness—she avoided flying with the flock, struggled during flight, and lost agility. Recognizing these early indicators, I promptly introduced calcium supplementation into her chop. Remarkably, within a week, Maui showed noticeable improvement, and within a month, she fully recovered, returning to her normal state.

11. **Change in eating habits**: Changes in the bird's eating or drinking habits could be a sign of illness. If there are changes in eating habits along with other signs of illness, seek veterinary help.

12. **Vent blockage**: If droppings are adhering to the bird's vent, it might hint at a digestive infection. If the vent is blocked, clean it gently and seek veterinary help.

In case of any doubts or concerns about your bird's health, always consult an avian veterinarian promptly.

43. Sick parrot (AI)

Bathing Birds, Parrot Bath Essentials

To keep their feathers healthy, birds need to bathe or be sprayed with water regularly. This not only cleans feathers but also supports overall skin health. Most birds may benefit from bathing about once a week. However, during dry seasons when homes are heated or air conditioned, bathing twice a week may be better to compensate for reduced humidity.

44. Bathing cockatiel (AI)

There are several methods to introduce bathing to your bird, catering to their preferences and needs.

1. **Tap water**: Some birds will love to play with running tap water. The temperature needs to be checked and the water stream to be kept on low.

2. **Bath toys**: Some birds will bathe in bath toys. Splashing the water with your fingers might get them in the mood.

3. **Spray bottles**: If a bird refuses to bathe on its own, try a spray bottle with lukewarm water, testing the temperature on your hand first.

4. **Shower buddy**: Lastly, for birds that dislike spraying, consider bringing them into the shower. Even perched on a curtain rod, they'll benefit from the humid air. Always prioritize safety and be wary of the water temperature.

As a last resort, you can briefly spray your bird with water, even if it does not seem to enjoy it. In nature, birds get rained on whether they like it or not, and to maintain healthy, shiny plumage, they need to bathe regularly.

45.Hygrometer (AI)

Low humidity can cause dry, itchy skin in parrots, potentially leading to feather plucking. Most parrots originate near the equator where it's often humid. A humidifier can be used to increase the humidity to normal levels that parrots are accustomed to. A range between **40-60% humidity** is ideal. This level of moisture helps prevent mold and mildew growth while at the same time providing moisture to the birds. A hygrometer can measure the humidity levels in your room.

Parrot Fitness, Bird Exercise Essentials

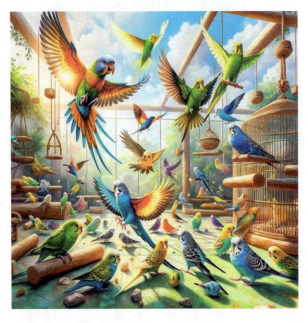

46. Parrot Fitness (AI)

Parrots are highly intelligent and active animals that require regular exercise to maintain their physical and mental well-being. As a responsible bird owner, it is important to encourage your feathered friend to engage in physical activity regularly. Here are some tips on encouraging exercise for your bird.

1. **Provide a spacious cage**: A bird's cage should be large enough to allow them to move around

freely and stretch their wings. Ensure that the cage is equipped with plenty of toys, perches, and swings to encourage your parrot to play and exercise.

2. **Schedule regular out-of-cage time:** Allow your bird to spend time outside their cage for at least a few hours each day. Provide a safe play area with toys, perches, and other enrichment items. Encourage your bird to fly around and explore their surroundings. I aim to let all my birds, including resident birds, out for about 6-8 hours a day.

3. **Offer a variety of toys:** Birds love to play with toys, and providing a variety of toys can keep them engaged and active. Offer toys that encourage physical activity such as swings, ladders, and climbing ropes. You can buy new toys online or try making DIY toys!

4. **Encourage foraging:** Birds love to forage for food, and providing opportunities for them to do so can encourage physical activity. Hide treats or food in various places around their play area, and encourage your bird to search for them, as this stimulates scenarios similar to the wild.

5. **Engage in interactive play:** Spend time playing with your bird to encourage exercise and mental stimulation. Play games such as fetch, hide and

seek, or a DIY game that only you and your bird know.

47. Exercise playground (AI)

Encouraging exercise for your pet bird is essential for their physical and mental well-being. Remember that in the wild they are uncaged and don't need to think about exercise as our domesticated birds do, since they fly for many miles.

Annual Vet Check, Health Exam Insights

48. Avian Vet (AI)

Comprehensive Physical Examination

During these visits, your veterinarian will record your bird's age, gender and origin. They'll also note details about your bird's diet, supplements, environment, past health issues, and recent interactions with other birds.

During the check-up, your bird's weight and overall health, including its eyes, ears, nares, beak, oral cavity, choana, neck, crop, pectoral muscles, wings, feathers, abdomen, vent, legs, feet, spine, and preen gland, will be examined.

The veterinarian will evaluate the heart, lungs, and air sacs. Possible diagnostic tests for birds include fecal analysis to inspect droppings for changes and parasites, blood tests to assess organ function, and additional tests such as psittacosis, gender determination, chlamydiosis, microbial tests, viral screenings, X-rays, and vaccinations.

Annual Checkups

I've had a veterinarian in Toronto tell me to come in twice a year for a check-up and I've also had another veterinarian also in Toronto tell me more frankly that I can skip a year or two because my birds are young and healthy.

Throughout the book, I've consistently advocated for following your veterinarian's recommendations as I generally support professional veterinary care, but the differing advice I received from 2 different veterinarians highlighted to me that veterinarians may have incentives for recommending more frequent visits.

Birds often hide symptoms of disease, so annual checkups are important for early identification and management of potential health issues.

Journeys Unfeathered, Traveling With Birds

As much as we love our feathered friends, there are times when we need to travel and cannot bring them along. During such times, bird boarding becomes a necessity.

Bird boarding refers to the temporary care of your bird while you are away from home. There are several options available for bird owners when it comes to boarding their birds, and choosing the right one can be daunting at first. I take care of birds for others when they travel so I can discuss the options available to bird owners.

Trusted Friend & Family

The first go-to option for bird boarding is to leave your bird with a **trusted friend or family member**. I do this with my family when I have to go overseas as I am lucky to have bird lovers in the family. This can be a good choice if you have a friend or family member who is experienced in caring for birds and has a safe and secure home environment for your bird. This is an option that provides peace of mind, knowing that your bird is being cared for by someone you trust.

However, the downside is that it's rare to find people we know who are experienced with parrots and available to care for our birds. I've seen many bird owners go through the risks and benefits of handing off their birds to family or friends. The birds may not have cage time out and if they do, they likely will not spend much time out as it's rare for a family member or friend to have a spare 4-6 hours a day.

God forbid, if something happens to your bird, someone new to birds will not be able to pick up the signs or may not know what to do. You also have to consider if they have any other pets like cats or dogs which may pose a risk to your bird. The benefit is that it is usually financially beneficial.

Bird Boarding Facility

Another option is to board your bird at a **bird boarding facility**. Many veterinary clinics and pet stores offer bird boarding services. These facilities offer a safe and secure environment for your bird, and they are staffed with experienced professionals who are knowledgeable about bird care.

Some facilities offer individual cages for each bird, while others offer group boarding options. I have only heard of such options anecdotally and I have no personal experience. I've been told that the birds may not get cage time out or status updates. Financially, this option is one of the more expensive approaches to boarding due to the overhead and staffing costs of boarding facilities.

49. Boarding Facility (AI)

Bird Boarding at Home

In addition to traditional boarding facilities, there are also **bird home-boarding** options. These bird caretakers may or may not be designed exclusively for birds but should be experienced in providing birds with a safe and comfortable environment in the comfort of their own home.

Using references or reviews may be the easiest way to identify the reliability of the providers. I, personally, fall into this category as I board parrots in my home along with my own flock. The benefits are that there aren't overhead expenses such as those found in commercial boarding facilities, and it may be a better financial option.

Furthermore, boarding facilities such as veterinary clinics and pet stores have operating hours, meaning that outside of business hours, *there's nobody with the birds*. At home-boarding, there is no separation of work and home, and the birds are with human companions nearby *all day long*.

Although I can't vouch for others that do this, cage time out is a priority, and so is updating the bird owners so they still feel connected to their feathered friend while traveling.

50. Home Boarding (AI)

House Visits Boarding

Lastly, one of the newer options in bird boarding is **house visits bird sitting services**. These services involve a professional bird sitter who comes to your home to care for your bird while you are away. This option is ideal for birds that may not tolerate being moved from their home environment, and it provides a familiar setting for your bird while you are away.

I have considered this option once but personally was not comfortable with providing someone access to my home. Home visits are a pricier option and require the service provider to be reputable.

No matter which option you choose, it is important for you to research and choose a reputable bird sitter. You should also provide clear instructions on your bird's dietary and medical needs, as well as any specific care instructions to ensure that your bird receives proper care and attention while you are away.

Eventually, every bird owner needs to travel and may not be able to take their bird along. Bird boarding is an important consideration for bird owners when traveling. Whether you choose a trusted friend or family member, a traditional boarding facility, home-based boarding, or an in-home parrot-sitting service, it is crucial to choose a reputable and experienced caretaker for your beloved bird. You will be grateful for the peace of mind knowing that your feathered friend is receiving the best possible care while you are away.

Parrot Gender Reveal, How to Identify Your Bird's Gender

Identifying your bird's gender can be a bit tricky, but let's simplify it. There are physical and behavioral clues that can provide hints about your bird's gender.

Physical Hints:

Size: Often but not always, male parrots are bigger than females.

Colors & Patterns: For example, male eclectus parrots typically display vibrant green plumage, while females are characterized by their red coloring.

Cere Coloration: The cere is the fleshy part located above the beak, housing the nostrils. Typically, adult male budgies have a blue cere, while adult females generally have a brownish-white cere. However, young budgies often have similar cere colors, which change as they mature.

Behavioral Hints:

Vocal Patterns: Sometimes, male parrots sing more

intricate tunes than females.

Nesting: Female parrots might show nesting behaviors such as shredding paper.

Mating Displays: Male parrots might dance or bow more often to attract partners.

Nevertheless, not all birds exhibit these behaviors. To deepen your bond with your feathered companion, understanding their gender may help. If you're still uncertain, consider DNA testing, which is the most precise way to determine your bird's gender.

I had long believed that Miko, my lovely conure, was a boy. However, as she grew older, I began to notice mixed behaviors that seemed to signal both genders. I decided to send a DNA test, which confirmed that she was indeed a female. It took months to adjust, but it certainly explained some of the behaviors I had observed!

I now offer DNA testing in downtown Toronto to all bird owners who want to confirm their bird's gender.

6. BEHAVIOR & TRAINING

"Whenever I take Miko, with her harness, for a walk-through Toronto's warm streets, she always attracts attention and everyone turns their heads in admiration."

My friends are always fascinated when they see my conure, Miko, cuddling with me on the sofa. It's like a party trick. Additionally, whenever I walk Miko through Toronto's warm streets with her harness, she draws a lot of attention, turning heads and gathering admiration from everyone we pass.

51. Miko and Samantha at Harborfront in Toronto

We reached this stage of closeness over time, and our bond and trust developed slowly. It is a very rewarding relationship that I wish for others to experience as well. You too can train your bird and bond closer.

Unlocking Trust, Hand Training New Parrots

Hand training a new parrot is an important process that can help build trust and establish a positive relationship between you and your feathered friend. I have broken hand training down to seven steps to follow patiently.

1. Creating a Safe Environment

Before you start hand training your bird, it's important to create a safe and comfortable environment for it. Make sure your bird's cage is spacious and well-equipped with toys, perches, and food and water dishes. Place the cage in a quiet area of your home, away from loud noises and other pets.

2. Building Trust

Building trust is the foundation of hand training your bird. Spend time near your bird's cage, talking to it in a calm and soothing voice. Offer your bird treats, such as small pieces of fruit or nuts, from outside the cage. Over time, your bird will begin to associate you with positive experiences and will become more comfortable with your presence.

3. Introducing Your Hand

Once your bird is comfortable with your presence, it's time to introduce your hand. Place your hand outside the cage, near your bird, and wait for your bird to approach. Don't force your hand into the cage or toward your bird. Instead, let your bird approach your hand on its own terms.

4. Using Positive Reinforcement

When your bird approaches your hand, offer a treat and praise your bird with a gentle voice. Repeat this process several times a day, gradually moving your hand closer to your bird each time. Over time, your bird will learn to associate your hand with positive experiences and will become more comfortable with being close to you.

5. Starting Target Training

Target training is a technique that involves teaching your bird to touch a specific object, like a stick or a clicker, with its beak. This technique can help build trust and establish a positive relationship between you and your bird. To start target training, place a small stick or clicker near your bird's cage and wait for your bird to approach it. When your bird touches the stick or clicker with its beak, offer a treat and praise your bird with a gentle voice.

6. Moving Outside the Cage

Once your bird is comfortable with your hand and target training, it's time to move outside the cage. Open the cage door and place your hand inside, near your bird. Offer treats and praise your bird when it approaches your hand. Over time, your bird will become more comfortable with being outside the cage and interacting with you.

7. Repeating and Reinforcing

Hand training your bird is a process that requires patience and consistency. Repeat these steps several times a day, every day, until your bird is comfortable with your hand and interacting with you outside the cage. Continue to use positive reinforcement.

52. Hand tamed budgie (AI)

Hand training your bird will help build trust and establish a stronger relationship between you and your beloved bird. The younger you start, the more malleable the bird will be. With patience and consistency, you can build a strong bond with your feathered friend that will last a lifetime.

Mastering the Leash, Harness Training Birds

53. Harnessed African grey (AI)

In some rare circumstances, with a well-trained and happy bird, you might be able to train a parrot to wear a harness and take them out for walks, just like dogs!

As easy as it may look, it may take months and perhaps years of training a parrot to wear the harness, let alone take them out with it on a leash.

On the other hand, there are times when a bird is tame enough that they can be taught to wear a harness in a couple of weeks.

From my own experience with harness training my conure Miko, it took me about one month to get her comfortable with the harness, and an additional two to three months to comfortably take her outside. It was relatively fast to train her because I started her young, and we already had an established bond. Before you can truly succeed with harness training, you must have a good bond with your bird.

There are four stages with harness training your bird.

1. Positive Association with Harness

Like with anything new and foreign to your bird, it's no surprise that your bird may be afraid of the new object, especially if you intend to have it on your bird! Firstly, make sure your bird is completely comfortable with the presence of the harness before even attempting to put it on them.

This might take a while, but patience is a virtue. Spend five to ten minutes a day to show your bird the harness, showing that it won't bring any harm to them. Always reward with their favorite treat when they display a behavior that you'd like. Eventually, try putting the treat in the loop where your bird's head would be to put the harness on, but don't put it on them yet! You want to make sure that they willingly take the treat through the harness before strapping them in. When putting the harness on, you may need to spread the wings so as to not cover the wings.

At the end of this process, you should be able to comfortably put the harness on your bird with their consent. This will take you into the next stage of harness training. Miko gets comfortable in the harness and doesn't freak out, but she still doesn't like the harness.

2. Positive Association with Leash

The leash also needs to be familiarized with before you can put it on the harness and take your bird out. When I harness trained Miko, she was very fearful of the leash and sometimes still is. Notably, attaching the leash to the harness tends to be much easier than fitting the harness onto your bird.

3. Building Trust with Your Bird on the Leash, indoors!

You've successfully put the harness and the leash on for the first time, wonderful, but then you get those questions and thoughts as I first did:

1. *What if my bird gets loose off the leash?*

2. *What if my bird flies off me and keeps jerking on the leash?*

3. *What if my bird absolutely HATES his experience outside with me?*

These are just a few of the concerns I had while harness-training Miko. That's why it's important to build trust and start with indoor harness and leash training. This approach not only allows your bird to grow comfortable wearing the harness in a safe environment but also helps you gain confidence in managing your bird before it's time to go outside!

I began with small steps for Miko - taking her to different parts of my condo, like the bedroom, bathroom, and kitchen, with the harness on her and leash in hand, while she remained perched on my finger. Whenever she stayed calm and comfortable with me, I rewarded her with her favorite treats. Initially, your bird might attempt to fly and panic upon realizing they are restrained by the harness. It's important to soothe them and allow for breaks if needed, before resuming the process. If your bird becomes overly stressed, it's best to end the training session and try again another day.

4. Taking Your Bird Outside!

The last and best part of the harness training process is successfully taking your bird outside! You've been practicing and training for this very moment. You definitely want to be prepared for a successful trip out. Here are seven items I always bring along for outdoor excursions with Miko.

1. **Harness and leash** on the bird.

2. **Your bird** of course!

3. **Their daily food**, such as pellets or seeds, for extended outings.

4. **Water bottle**

5. **Small dishes** to serve food and water during breaks.

6. **Treats** for rewarding good behavior.

7. **A carrier,** like a bird backpack, for giving your bird and your hands and shoulders a break from time to time. It's also useful for storing all the other items.

54. Miko in a harness

From Beak to Heart, Strengthening the Parrot-Human Bond

Developing a strong bond with parrots is not as easy as it is with dogs. Parrots do not have the same long history of domestication, and being prey animals, they often find it difficult to form strong bonds. However, establishing a strong bond with your parrot can be equally as rewarding as with a dog, if not more.

55. Miko, Apollo and Pettu

Parrots are beautiful animals that require some time to gain trust and develop the bond on their terms. When you successfully bond with your parrot, the amount of happiness is immeasurable.

One random day while relaxing with your bird, you will spontaneously realize how much you love them and how reciprocal they are. I, myself had this realization on the couch and took the picture of both of us shown above.

It definitely is worth it for bird owners to invest the time in bonding with their parrots, so they can establish that incredible relationship with them.

How can I form a strong bond with my parrot?

Just like how people bond over dinner or lunch, you can bond with your parrot over food. Here are two ideas incorporating food.

1. **Hand feed your bird's favorite snack**: My conure, Miko, loves apples, so I cut up a few and give them to him in moderation. Before I discovered his irresistible attraction to apples, I used to let him eat seeds from my hand.

2. **Let your bird join you for dinner**: As long as you're eating parrot-safe foods, you can feast together and bond just like humans do. Bonding over mealtime is an effective way of developing a bond with your parrot.

Spending time together is another way to win them over. It can be passive or active time together. Here are five ideas.

1. **Passive bonding**: Let your bird passively sit on your shoulder while you're doing what you normally do.

2. **Play games**: Actively engage with your bird using toys. The possibilities are endless, and games are often improvised based on your bird's reactions.

3. **Cuddle with your bird:** Parrots, much like other pets, often seek physical affection. There will be times when they come up to you and press against your face to feel your warmth.

56. Miko getting cozy

This act of snuggling can be a profound way of strengthening your bond. Similarly, you can gently hold them in your hands, allowing them to sit comfortably and feel secure. This kind of physical closeness not only provides comfort to your bird but also fosters a deeper emotional connection between you and your beloved bird.

4. **Head scratches**: Most birds willingly accept head scratches, and some will never want you to stop!

5. **Shower together**: As long as the water temperature is not too extreme, you can shower and spend time together soaking up water.

All these efforts will strengthen the bond you share with your parrot. Every day, you'll be bonding, so you must be careful because a single moment of mistrust could reverse the bond you've developed.

Lastly, be aware of cues that your bird isn't comfortable with a given activity. These cues are easy to recognize, such as opening its beak as if to bite, actual biting, or backing away from you. It's important to respect their comfort zone and try again later.

When I cuddle with my conure, Miko, late at night, it's hit or miss. Sometimes Miko is cranky, and other times very affectionate. I listen to Miko's mood, and that's how we've built our strong bond."

7. BIRD GROOMING

"It's natural to wonder why wild birds don't need grooming while domesticated birds do."

Birds may require grooming for various reasons, ranging from health concerns like an overgrown beak to personal comfort issues, such as when their nails become too long and start digging into your skin. It's natural to wonder why wild birds don't need grooming while domesticated birds do.

The answer lies in their different lifestyles and environments. In the wild, birds naturally wear down their beaks and nails through daily activities, which isn't always possible for pet birds in a home setting. I have experience grooming over a hundred different parrots of various species multiple times. Now, let me guide you through the three types of grooming that are essential for bird care: nail clipping, wing trimming, and beak trimming.

◆◆◆

Avian Pedicure, Nail Clipping Birds

57. Nail clipping with clippers without towel retrain (AI)

Clipping a bird's nails is the most common grooming request I get from bird owners. Nail clipping not only prevents the nails from digging into your skin or snagging on your clothing but also significantly improves your bird's health if your bird has excessively long nails. Long nails can be a sign of using the wrong perch size or material, leading to insufficient natural wear. If the perch is not suitable for the bird, their nails won't wear down as they normally would, leading to overgrowth.

Short nails make it much easier for your bird to move around, climb, and perch comfortably. In the wild, birds naturally wear down their nails through various activities, but in a domestic setting, this may not be possible. Therefore, nail clipping may be needed.

In order to successfully clip your bird's nails, you should have the following items on hand.

1. **Styptic powder,** such as Kwik Stop, or alternatively flour or cornstarch.

2. **A hand towel**, or a small blanket.

3. **Specialized bird clippers,** or small human nail clippers for cutting small parrot nails.

4. **A small dremel.**

It can be an anxious task to clip your bird's nails, so follow this step-by-step guide on how to trim your bird's nails for the best results.

Have styptic powder or flour ready

It's very easy to trim your bird's nails too deep and cut into something called *the quick* – the vein in a bird's nails. No matter how careful you may be, accidents do happen. Your bird might panic and kick its feet while you're in the midst of clipping the nail. Birds are fragile and relatively small creatures, so blood loss can be extremely dangerous. Always have styptic powder, cornstarch, or flour handy whenever you groom your bird. It helps to wet a Q-tip and dab the styptic powder onto it before applying it to your bird's nail. Alternatively, you could use your fingers to pinch the styptic powder onto the nail if needed.

Always use a small towel to restrain

Whether you have an untamed bird or the sweetest little feathered friend, even the most obedient birds can become afraid of nail trimming. Cover your bird with a towel during nail trimming to reduce your pet's anxiety and make the nail clipping more successful. Using a towel also improves your grip on your bird, enabling you to properly restrain them and prevent excessive movement.

Trim only the tip of your bird's nail

When cutting a bird's nails, you should aim to trim only the sharp point of the nail, avoiding the quick. It can be quite difficult to locate the quick, so the best approach is to be conservative. I typically use a dremel to shave down the nails and reserve the clippers only for very long nails where the quicks are easily identifiable.

Work quickly but carefully

Let's face the facts: no bird enjoys getting their nails clipped, and no human enjoys doing it to their birds! To reduce stress for both you and your pet, work quickly to trim the nails and then release your pet. Being restrained in a towel and held down is no fun for any bird. So, if you notice your bird is in distress, release them and try again later.

Talk softly to your bird

Don't forget to talk softly to your bird, keeping your voice lighthearted and reassuring. Hearing your voice may help them calm down a bit as you work on clipping their nails.

By keeping these tips in mind, you can help make nail trimming a much smoother experience for both you and your feathered friend.

Now that you know the approach to nail clipping, remember, you don't necessarily have to do it yourself if you're not comfortable. Neither one of us wants your beloved bird to get injured. Consider getting their nails clipped by a local veterinarian or a reputable bird expert.

Flight Control, Wing Trimming Birds

58. Wing clipping without towel retrain (AI)

Clipping your bird's wings can be an intimidating task, and it definitely requires a lot of patience and practice to succeed. In the wrong hands, wing clipping can be risky and can cause pain and permanent damage to your pet bird. However, if you decide to proceed at your own risk, having a steady hand and following these steps carefully may help you mitigate any potential hazards.

Note: I would advise that if you do decide to clip your pet bird's wings, it should only be for the purposes of safety or training. I am a strong believer that all birds should have the ability to fly, and I only recommend wing clipping in cases where your bird is prone to accidents while flying, or if you need a period of time to properly train your pet bird without the risk of them flying away in fright. Nonetheless, clipping your bird's wings is your choice - I just hope that you decide to do it for plausible reasons!

I clipped Miko's virgin wings once, and I regretted it. This happened when I moved to a new condo; I was concerned about her safety and also wanted to bond more with her. I did a full clip, meaning all her flight feathers were trimmed. Normally, I opt for a partial clip where the bird can still partially fly. It took Miko over six months to regain her ability to fly, and during that time, she gained weight. She missed out on her usual exercise and lost confidence in flying. It was a long journey of retraining to get her to fly again. Even now, I don't think she has regained the full agility she once had.

How to clip your bird's wings

By following these steps, you can learn to safely clip your own bird's wings at home. However, if you are unsure about your ability to safely clip your bird's wings, or if you become nervous even in the middle of doing a trim, it's always best to stop.

Have your bird first aid kit ready

Regardless of whether you are confident in clipping your bird's wings or have done it before, accidents can happen! Before you begin, ensure that your bird first aid kit is nearby and ready in preparation for any unexpected incidents. Having quick access to medical supplies is crucial in case an accident occurs during the clipping process.

Pick a relaxed, quiet location

Location is key when you're preparing to clip your bird's wings; it's important to pick a space where your bird will remain as calm as possible. Opt for an area away from your bird's cage, preferably somewhere with minimal household noise or exposure to loud, sudden sounds. A space like a spare bedroom or bathroom is ideal, as it reduces the likelihood of your bird becoming jumpy or aggressive during the wing clipping process.

I do all my grooming in my bathroom, where there are no distractions and where all my supplies are readily available.

Seek help if necessary

It's a good idea to have a friend or family member help restrain your bird for you while you do the trimming. Many accidents occur when individuals try to work on birds that are not properly restrained, so having a partner assist you during the clipping will significantly reduce the chance of accidents.

Use a towel to restrain your bird

Using a towel to restrain your bird not only ensures their comfort but also their security while you trim their flight feathers. It reduces the likelihood of you getting bitten or scratched and decreases the chance of your bird escaping from your grasp, jumping, or twisting free. Additionally, using a towel helps associate the experience with the towel rather than your hand, maintaining a safe and positive relationship with your bird.

Cut only the primary flight feathers

Generally, the most widely accepted, efficient, and effective method is to clip only the first three to five primary flight feathers on each of your bird's wings. When trimming the feathers, ensure you use sharp scissors and avoid cutting into feather shafts that appear dark in color. A dark feather shaft indicates a 'blood feather', which can lead to serious problems if broken or cut. The more feathers you cut, the more your bird's ability to fly will be impaired.

59. Flight feathers clipped

The recovery phase

When you have finished clipping your bird's wings, it's important to let your pet bird rest in its cage. Wing clippings can be stressful, so allowing them some time to recuperate is essential.

Flight feathers will grow back during the next molt after being trimmed. Partially trimmed flight feathers do not completely prevent your bird from flying. Instead, your bird should be able to glide and safely land on the floor.

In summary, wing clip at your own risk or seek professional help. Here are the benefits and risks to help you make an informed decision.

The benefits

1. Minimizing the risk of injury, such as collisions with windows, for birds that fly freely in the house.

2. Allowing birds to play safely outside their cage, although this may not always protect them from pets or children that pose a threat.

3. Decreasing the possibility of escape, such as flying out through an open door.

4. Lowering aggression in a dominant bird.

The risks

1. Harm from crash landing.

2. Psychological issues like phobias and feather picking.

3. Risking injury during the clipping process.

4. Inability to escape predator attacks.

Trimming the Curve, Beak Trimming Birds

Beak trimming for your bird can seem intimidating, but it's essential for some birds. A bird's beak is made of keratin and grows continuously throughout its life. Therefore, it needs to be regularly ground down, either naturally through the bird's activities or with a beak trim.

60. Dremel ready to beak trim without towel restrain (AI)

Bird beak maintenance

In most cases, a healthy bird's daily activities will help naturally keep the beak ground down and at its optimal shape and size. These activities include foraging, chewing, and eating. Generally, birds like to rub their beaks on rough surfaces, which also helps mitigate the beak's shape and size.

Providing items such as natural wood perches and cuttlebones can keep bird beaks in good shape. Nuts and other hard, safe foods for birds would also help with the natural wear and tear of the bird's beak.

On rare occasions, a bird's beak might become overgrown or oddly shaped. Often, overgrown beaks are due to some type of injury that has happened in the past, certain medical conditions in birds, or the bird's lifestyle, which prevents the natural wear of the beak. Therefore, a beak trim done by you, or someone experienced may be needed.

The beak trimming process

Unless you're experienced, never attempt to trim your bird's beak yourself. Doing so could pose a risk of injury to both you and your pet.

If you notice your bird's beak looks too long, or abnormal in any shape, your first step should be to schedule an appointment with an avian veterinarian. They will need to thoroughly diagnose your bird to determine the cause of the beak abnormality. In some situations, you may also need to address an underlying medical condition in addition to having the veterinarian perform a beak trim for you.

When your bird gets a beak trim, a dremel is typically used for precise grinding. Doing so this way mimics the natural wear and grinding of the beak during a bird's regular activities. In cases where the beak is excessively long, a combination of a clipper and a dremel may be used.

61. Maicu

The picture above features a conure with an overgrown beak, a bird who visited Bird Sitting Toronto in 2023 for a beak trim. It's clearly visible that the beak has grown excessively long and needs to be trimmed down.

Once the beak trimming is completed, your bird is often quite stressed after the session. It's best to return your bird home and place their cage in a quiet, dim space. It may also help to reassure your bird in a calm voice but avoid excessive interaction outside of this. Generally, a bird wants to be left alone after a visit to the veterinarian or after a grooming. Be sure to provide any food and water that it needs and let your bird return to its normal demeanor on its own after the grooming is complete.

8. SUPPORTIVE PRODUCTS

"I often encounter bird owners who are seeking help to rehome their birds, and the common reason is that they no longer have the time to properly care for them."

I always recommend finding more convenient ways to take care of your bird. This approach not only eases the day-to-day tasks but also provides you with more quality time to spend with your bird, focusing on bonding and enjoyment rather than on the chores associated with them.

I often encounter bird owners who are seeking help to rehome their birds, and the common reason is that they no longer have the time to properly care for them. To prevent this heartbreaking scenario, I advocate for proactive measures. I recommend two products that I personally use and have found them to simplify bird care.

The goal is to reduce the time and effort required for routine maintenance, allowing you and your feathered friend more time for interaction and play.

Caring for your beloved birds shouldn't feel like a burden; with the right tools and approach, it can be a joyful and fulfilling experience.

Air Filter

62. Air filter in a room full of birds (AI)

Parrots, with their sensitive respiratory systems, are particularly vulnerable to poor air quality. With the intention of safeguarding their health, I use a HEPA air filter I bought from Amazon in their room. HEPA filters can trap smaller particles, which standard filters might miss, thereby offering better protection.

Though we can never be certain if the HEPA filter completely shields our birds from invisible pathogens in the air, I consider it a small, worthwhile investment for the safety and well-being of my birds.

If you've noticed a distinct bird scent in the room, the air filter can also help mitigate this. *Bird dander*, which includes feathers, feather dust, and other particles shed by birds, can become a significant concern. When birds preen, flap their wings, or engage in other activities, they spread dander throughout the environment. This can be particularly troublesome for people with asthma or lung conditions, as it may trigger allergic-like symptoms such as sneezing or coughing.

In addition to these activities, parrots release dander when cleaning themselves, flying, or even defecating. This fine dander can enter our lungs, triggering respiratory symptoms. To mitigate this, using a dedicated air purifier in the bird's room can improve air quality and reduce allergy symptoms. It's important to choose a purifier that meets HEPA standards and is free from ozone production or ionizing features, as these can be harmful to birds' delicate respiratory systems.

Regular vacuuming is key to maintaining a dust-free environment. Enhance your bird cage cleaning routine by diligently wiping down surfaces and frequently replacing cage liners. Opt for rooms with floorboards over carpets, as they are easier to clean, and consider furnishings that are simpler to maintain, like leather sofas and plastic curtains or blinds. For those particularly sensitive, wearing a face mask, such as an N95, during cleaning can provide extra protection.

In summary, keeping bird dander to a minimum is important for the health of both you and your pet bird. By getting a HEPA air filter, you are not only protecting yourself and other people in your home but also the birds themselves. When selecting an air purifier for your bird's room, choose one that works quietly to avoid causing your bird unnecessary stress.

Robot Vacuum

63. A robot vacuum in a room full of birds (AI)

As a bird owner, you're likely well-acquainted with the inevitable mess that comes with these charming pets. From feathers to food crumbs and droppings, maintaining a clean space for your bird can be quite a daunting task. That's why investing in a robot vacuum can be a game-changer for bird owners. A robot vacuum not only saves you precious time and effort but also ensures a clean and healthy environment for your bird.

Birds will leave feathers and droppings both around their cages and in their general living areas. This mess is not just unsightly; it can be unhealthy too. Bird droppings are a breeding ground for bacteria and pathogens, posing health risks to both you and your bird.

Cleaning up after your bird can be a time-consuming and tedious task. You may find yourself vacuuming or sweeping every day, multiple times a day to keep up with the mess. Enter the robot vacuum: a convenient solution that can be programmed to clean on a regular basis, effectively taking over the routine cleanup. This means less time spent cleaning and more time enjoying the company of your feathery friend.

One of the standout features of a robot vacuum is its ability to access hard-to-reach spots such as underneath furniture. Birds love perching in high places or tucked-away corners, areas that are often challenging for us to clean thoroughly. A robot vacuum can navigate difficult areas effortlessly, making sure that no spot is left untouched.

Besides keeping your bird's living area tidy, a robot vacuum also aids in maintaining better air quality. It helps contain the particles from bird droppings, reducing the likelihood of them becoming airborne and affecting your home's air quality, which is important for reducing the risk of respiratory issues.

> *I have 3 robot vacuums running multiple times a day. They have been an absolute game-changer, saving heaps of time tackling the mess of all the birds.*

It's important to note that while a robot vacuum does wonders in managing everyday mess, it's not a complete substitute for deep cleaning. You will still need to do your deep cleans. Lastly, while I won't be suggesting specific robot vacuum models or brands, as budgets and preferences vary, I do hope that sharing the benefits I've experienced might inspire you to consider this option. It's not about making affiliate earnings; it's about the value and time you could save, allowing you to enjoy more moments with your feathered companions.

CONCLUSION

As I come to the end of this journey, I can't help but feel a sense of accomplishment. Thank you for dedicating your time to learn about caring for birds. Sharing my knowledge and experience in this book has been a true honor, and I sincerely hope these pages have been both informative and helpful to you.

In the preceding chapters, we began by outlining the various types of parrots and then delved into their dietary needs and safety measures. We highlighted essential topics such as bird grooming and behavior training, providing insights for effective care. Our journey concluded with practical advice on convenient ways to care for your feathered friends.

Remember, quality time with your bird is invaluable! Caring for birds demands patience and commitment, but the joy it brings is unmatched. By offering better care and attention, you're ensuring a rich and fulfilling life for your beloved bird, which in turn enriches your own life with memorable moments.

As we close this chapter and you continue on your bird care journey, I invite you to stay connected and follow me on social media for more insights and updates. My Instagram handle is @birdsittingtoronto, and you can find more resources on my website at www.birdsittingtoronto.ca.

Lastly, if you've found this book helpful, please share it with other bird owners who might benefit from it. Together, let's keep learning, growing, and nurturing our feathered friends.

64. Samantha & BST Flock

About Bird Sitting Toronto

65. BST Services

I started Bird Sitting Toronto back in October 2021. My husband and I were going on a short trip to the United States, and we didn't have anyone to care for Miko, Mango, and Maui. I thought:

"Should I give them enough food and water for the duration of the trip and hope they're okay? What if they spill their bowls?"

I then looked for family members and friends to watch them, but they weren't familiar with birds and their care. I looked at Google and couldn't find any sitters besides those for dogs and cats. It then clicked to me that there must be a huge need for bird sitters - I know that birds aren't the most popular type of pet, but there are definitely bird owners out there experiencing the same issue as me. That's when I decided to create the service.

It started off by providing a loving second home for birds through boarding services, but as my passion and desire to care for each of my client's birds grew, I expanded the services to include grooming, such as nail and beak trimming, DNA sexing, and even bird rehoming. To ensure that birds have the best possible nutrition, we have also made many recipes of bird chop for our clients as well.

Upon your arrival at Bird Sitting Toronto, my husband and I will personally meet and greet you and your birds to ensure a smooth and stress-free check-in process. Prior to your arrival for drop-off, we take the time to get to know your birds and their unique needs, so we can provide the best care possible.

This can be done through an optional scheduled virtual call, allowing us to answer any questions you may have and meet your bird via video call. Alternatively, you can fill out a registration form and provide details about your bird to ensure we offer the best possible care.

We prioritize your birds' basic needs, such as ensuring that they have fresh water and food daily. We offer a variety of healthy diets to suit their dietary requirements, and we can cater to any specific dietary restrictions your birds may have - just let us know!

In addition to their basic needs, we understand that your birds need exercise and social interaction to stay healthy and happy. That's why we offer regular flight time for your birds to stretch their wings and get ample exercise. We also provide opportunities for them to play and interact with us, treating them as if they were our own.

To keep you informed and at ease, we provide daily reports and updates on your bird's well-being during their stay with us. We want you to know that they are receiving the best care possible while you are away.

Finally, we do ask for your permission to share photos and updates of your bird on our social media page, so other bird owners can appreciate and learn from your feathered friend. We understand that privacy is important, so we will respect your decision if you choose not to share.

66. Polaroids of birds boarding at BST

In summary, we provide world-class service for your birds during their stay with us. We prioritize their basic needs, provide ample space for exercise and social interaction, and keep you informed with daily updates. We strive to create a positive and enjoyable experience for your feathered friends while you are away.

Thank you to all our clients!

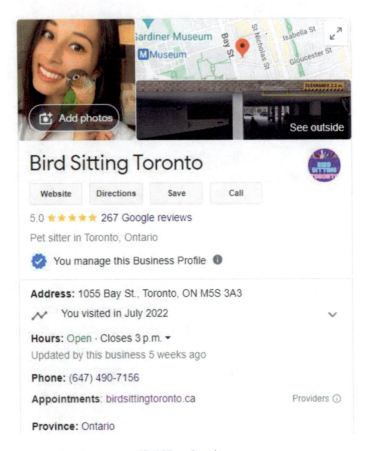

67. BST on Google

APPENDICES

Appendix A: Avian Veterinarian Resources

7 Avian Veterinarians in Toronto

Finding a veterinarian that can tend to your beloved bird in Toronto may seem difficult, especially since birds are the minority and most veterinarians commonly service dogs and cats.

I compiled a list of 7 veterinary clinics in Toronto that cater to your parrot's needs. To ensure accuracy, I contacted all local veterinarian clinics to confirm their services for parrots and included only those that do as of the start of 2023.

1. **Amherst Veterinary Hospital**

Location: 3206 Eglinton Ave E, Scarborough
Phone: 416-261-3322
Website: www.amherstvh.com

2. **Animal Hospital of High Park**

Location: 325 Weston Rd UNIT 3A, Toronto
Phone: 416-763-4200
Website: www.animalhospitalhighpark.com

3. **Bathurst Animal Hospital**

Location: 352 Wilson Avenue, Toronto
Phone: 416-634-9090
Website: www.petdoctor.ca

4. **Greenwood Park Animal Hospital**

Location: 1041 Gerrard St E, Toronto
Phone: 416-778-6666
Website: www.greenwoodpah.ca

5. **Riverdale Animal Hospital**

Location: 901 Danforth Ave, Toronto
Phone: 416-465-4655
Website: www.theriverdaleanimalhospital.com

6. **South Etobicoke Animal Hospital**

Location: 741 The Queensway, Etobicoke
Phone: 416-201-9123
Website: www.tdvg.ca

7. **The Links Road Animal & Bird Clinic**

Location: 41 The Links Rd, Toronto
Phone: 416-223-1165
Website: www.thelinksroadanimalclinic.com

I take my pet birds to the **Links Road Animal & Bird Clinic**, which is the most popular veterinarian among my clients in Toronto. I don't have any affiliation with them; I've just received the best service there for my beloved birds.

68. Vets in Toronto

Appendix B: Educational Resources

The Association of Avian Veterinarians Educational Brochures

This appendix consists of a curated collection of educational brochures from the Association of Avian Veterinarians. These resources offer valuable insights into various aspects of avian care, ranging from health and nutrition to behavior and emergency preparedness. They serve as an essential guide for any parrot owner seeking comprehensive and reliable information for the well-being of their feathered companions.

1. **Avian Chlamydiosis and Psittacosis**: https://birdsittingtoronto.ca/wp-content/uploads/2022/09/AAV_Veterinary-Care-for-Your.pdf

2. **Veterinary Care for Your Pet Parrots**: https://birdsittingtoronto.ca/wp-content/uploads/2022/09/AAV_Veterinary-Care-for-Your.pdf

3. **Basic Care for Companion Parrots:** https://birdsittingtoronto.ca/wp-content/uploads/2022/09/AAV_Basic-Care-for-Companion.pdf

4. **Behavior: Normal and Abnormal:** https://birdsittingtoronto.ca/wp-content/uploads/2022/09/behavior.pdf

5. **Digital Scales:** https://birdsittingtoronto.ca/wp-content/uploads/2022/09/AAV-Digital-Scales.pdf

6. **Feather Loss:** https://birdsittingtoronto.ca/wp-content/uploads/2022/09/feather-loss-cause-and-treatment.pdf

7. **Feeding Parrots:** https://birdsittingtoronto.ca/wp-content/uploads/2022/09/feeding-birds.pdf

8. **Injury Prevention and Emergency Care:** https://birdsittingtoronto.ca/wp-content/uploads/2022/09/injury-prevention-and-emergency-care.pdf

9. **Signs of Illness in Companion Parrots:** https://birdsittingtoronto.ca/wp-content/uploads/2022/09/AAV_Signs-of-Illness-in-Comp.pdf

10. **Ultraviolet Lighting for Companion Parrots:** https://birdsittingtoronto.ca/wp-content/uploads/2022/09/UV-lighting.pdf

11. **When Should I Take My Parrot to a Veterinarian:** https://birdsittingtoronto.ca/wp-content/uploads/2022/09/AAV_When-to-visit-a-vet_2020.pdf

Resources

Veterinary Resources

Pets and Vets (2017). Avian health exam. https://petsandvets.ca/files/2017/02/Avian-health-exam.pdf

Bird-Vet. Setting up your bird's cage. https://www.bird-vet.com/Settingupyourbirdscage.aspx

VCA Canada. Teflon (polytetrafluoroethylene) poisoning in birds. https://vcacanada.com/know-your-pet/teflon-polytetrafluoroethylene-poisoning-in-birds

The Links Road Animal Clinic. Pet health articles. https://thelinksroadanimalclinic.com/pet-health-resources/pet-health-articles/articles/?rid=801

VCA Canada. Veterinary care for your bird - annual exam. https://vcacanada.com/know-your-pet/veterinary-care-for-your-bird---annual-exam

Brisbane Bird and Exotics Veterinary Service (BBEVS). Signs of illness in birds. https://bbevs.com.au/signs-of-illness-in-birds/

Merck Veterinary Manual. Signs of illness in pet birds. https://www.merckvetmanual.com/bird-owners/routine-care-and-breeding-of-birds/signs-of-illness-in-pet-birds

VCA Canada. Leg bands and identification for birds. https://vcacanada.com/know-your-pet/leg-bands-and-identification

The Association of Avian Veterinarians Educational Brochures

Internet Resources

Learn Bird Care. Home page. https://www.learnbirdcare.com/

The Happy Chicken Coop. Small pet birds. https://www.thehappychickencoop.com/small-pet-birds/

Everything Birds Online. Comprehensive weaning guide. https://everythingbirdsonline.com/comprehensive-weaning-guide/

Parrots Canada. Home page. http://www.parrotscanada.com/

PetCoach. Vomiting and regurgitation in birds: common causes.

https://www.petcoach.co/article/vomiting-and-regurgitation-in-birds-common-causes/

Bird Sitting Toronto. https://birdsittingtoronto.ca/

Fun Time Birdy. The 4 types of bird toys your parrot must have. https://www.funtimebirdy.com/the-4-types-of-bird-toys-your-parrot-must-have.html

OpenAI. DALL-E 3 Image Generation Model. 2023. https://chat.openai.com/chat

Books

Conures by Carol Frischman

Parrot Secrets. Bonus health book [PDF]. https://www.parrotsecrets.com/

Greg Harrison, DVM, Dipl ABVP-Avian, Dipl ECAMS, and Teresa Lightfoot, DVM, Dipl ABVP-Avian. Clinical Avian Medicine. https://avianmedicine.net/publication_cat/clinical-avian-medicine

Manufactured by Amazon.ca
Bolton, ON